GRAMERCY GREAT MASTERS

Gustav Klimt

Gramercy Books
New York • Avenel

Acknowledgments
The publishers would like to thank the museums for reproduction permission
and in particular the **BRIDGEMAN ART LIBRARY** for their help in supplying
the illustrations for the book.

Gemaldegalerie, Dresden: Beech Wood I.
Historisches Museum der Stadt, Vienna: Fable; Idyll; The Auditorium of the
Old Castle Theater; Pallas Athena; Emilie Flöge.
Kunsthistorisches Museum, Vienna: Love.
Musée d'Orsay, Paris: Roses Among the Trees.
Museo d'Arte Moderna, Venice: Judith II.
Neue Galerie, Linz: Portrait of a Lady; Full-Face Portrait of a Lady.
Narodni Galerie, Prague: Portrait of a Young Woman.
Österreichisches Galerie, Vienna: Water Snakes I (Friends); Country Garden
with Sunflowers; Sonia Knips; Fritza Riedler; The Kiss; Judith I.
Private collection: Portrait of a Young Woman; Franz Schubert at the Piano.
Zentralsparkasse-Bank, Vienna: Water Nymphs.

Published by Gramercy Books
a division of Random House Value Publishing, Inc.
40 Engelhard Avenue
Avenel, New Jersey 07001

Printed and bound in Italy

ISBN 0-517-18225-4

10 9 8 7 6 5 4 3 2

Gustav Klimt
His Life and Works

The end of a century always engenders great anticipation of what will occur in the next hundred years combined with an apprehensive fear of the unknown. From critics to spiritualists, social scientists to ordinary folk, everyone sees in the decade before and after the turn of the century an echo of their own doubts and expectations.

The fin de siècle, the period encompassing the last decade of the nineteenth century and the first decade of the twentieth, was no exception, particularly in Germany and Austria, where politics, art, and social conditions were in flux.

The glorious, omnipresent Hapsburgs were still the mighty rulers, but their position was precarious. The members of the growing upper middle-class were becoming politically and socially strong; they wanted their voices to be heard in a democratic society. Ambiguity and the fears and doubts of this new class were the fuel for new artistic and social movements. It was at this time that Sigmund Freud changed the entire view of people's emotional lives with his theories of psychology. Emotion was freely expressed, splashed on canvas with color and verve in the style appropriately called Expressionism. Artistic realism was

Medicine
(detail)

overshadowed by a decorative style called Art Nouveau. It was a period of conflicting needs, desires, and symbols.

Gustav Klimt's life spans this fascinating and dramatic period. His art reflects its flux, the shift from the security of the nineteenth century to the anxiety of the twentieth. Vienna, his home, was one of the most brilliant and culturally active cities of the era. It was the capital of the Hapsburg Empire and home to Sigmund Freud, Gustav Mahler, and other creative luminaries. Indeed, it was in Vienna where new concepts in art, music, literature, and philosophy were forged.

Embodying this spirit of the era was the work of Gustav Klimt—his graceful arabesques with their hint of Byzantine mystery, his allegorical symbols charged with conflicting meaning, his unsettling landscapes, his erotic nude drawings. He was undoubtedly the most celebrated painter in the ferment of fin-de-siècle Vienna. His name was synonymous with all that was modern and avant-garde in art. Yet, when he died in 1918, his work seemed almost "old-fashioned," as if it belonged to another time. This relatively quick change in taste showed, more than anything else, that Klimt's life and work uniquely exemplified that turning point between the old and new, the end of an era and the beginning of all that was bold and new in European culture.

EARLY BEGINNINGS

Gustav Klimt was born on July 14, 1862, in Baumgarten, a suburb of Vienna. He was the second of seven children. His father, Ernst Klimt, was Bohemian, his mother, Anna, Viennese. Ernst was an engraver and a goldsmith who passed his love of art on to three of his children. Gustav and Ernst, Jr., born two years later in 1864, became painters. Georg, born in 1867, became a sculptor and engraver; he created many of the elaborate frames for his brothers' art.

After eight years at the local primary school, in 1876 Klimt entered the School of Applied Art on scholarship. His brothers Ernst and Georg followed a year later. The School of Applied Art was affiliated with the Royal and Imperial Austrian Museum for Art and Industry and was the first school of its kind in continental Europe. The school's faculty wanted to teach technique, practical skills, and knowledge; but in addition to simply displaying its students' art to the general public, it wanted to raise the level of taste in all areas of manufacturing and industry—from matchbook covers to ceilings, from advertising posters to menus.

Unfortunately, the school did not live up to its reputation—at least where the Klimt brothers were concerned. Although they studied under such important teachers as Michael Rieser, Karl Hrachowina, and Ludwig Minnigerode, they found that the school stifled their unique creativity. Instead of teaching a new vision, it kept the old alive. Quite simply, the school churned out artists who could copy an Egyptian sphinx or a Greek column to perfection, but not ones who could develop their own styles and views.

But Klimt did not complain—at first. Indeed, he was the only student at the school whose great artistic career was launched before his education was complete. He learned ornamental drawing. He copied three-dimensional and flat designs; he drew human figures; he learned everything he could regarding perspective and style. He did so well that he was promoted to a specialized painter's class with Ferdinand Laufberger.

Klimt's teachers—especially Michael Rieser—and the principal of the art school promoted his career. And, in 1876, Klimt received his first commission. Along with his brother, Ernst, and fellow classmate Franz Matsch, Klimt was asked to work with Rieser on some stained-glass windows in the Votive Church, the first large building to be constructed on the Ringstrasse. They did so well that the trio formed an artists' association, the Company of Artists; they were ready and eager to take on painting commissions while not in class.

THE RINGSTRASSE OPPORTUNITY

The three artists first found work with the architectural firm Fellner and Hellmer, who specialized in decorating and designing theaters. For them, they painted motifs, murals, and columns in theaters in Fiume, Bucharest, Reichenberg, and Karlsbad.

But it was not enough for this ambitious group. By 1884, they had been out of school one full year and they very much wanted more important commissions—which to the aspiring artists could only mean the Ringstrasse in the heart of the cultural capital of Vienna.

To that end, they wrote a letter to Rudolf von Eitelberger, the director of the School of Applied Arts. Their request began: "Until now, our activity . . . has mainly been directed at the provinces and abroad; it is therefore our dearest desire to carry out more extensive work in our native city, and it may be that an opportunity exists at this very moment, as Vienna's new monumental buildings are approaching completion and decorative artwork in these buildings is probably only accorded to their most significant parts, so that the most excellent artists are fully occupied."

The Company of Artists knew that fin-de-siècle Vienna was full of opportunity. They knew that construction on the massive government buildings, the academies, and the theaters that made up the magnificent Ringstrasse boulevards were almost finished—and that there was more than enough work for skilled decorative artists.

The trio's "dearest desire" was granted and, from 1886 to 1888, they tirelessly worked on the ceilings of the two stairways for the magnificent new Burgtheater. The murals Klimt painted included *The Chariot of Thespis*, *The Altar of Dionysus*, *The Globe Theater in London*, *The Theater of Taormina*, and *The Altar of Venus*—all of them composed along classic, realistic lines, all of them extolling the romance and grandeur of heroic thespian and mythological themes. The Emperor Franz Joseph was so pleased with his decorations for the new Burgtheater that he awarded Klimt with an Order of Merit for his work.

The group was also busy decorating the massive main entrance staircase at the Court Museum of Art History. Klimt had already begun working on the paintings between the columns and arches of the stairwell landings in 1879 when his teacher Ferdinand

Jurisprudence
(detail)

Laufberger asked for his help. Now, all three artists began on it in earnest. The staircase was a challenge for the young artists. Albert Ilg, the director of the applied arts collection in the Court Museum, wanted a celebration of the imperial family's generosity throughout the decades and, at the same time, a glorification of middle-class progress throughout the centuries. Ilg, a stickler for authenticity, envisioned this theme's execution through a series of paintings depicting cultural achievements from history, a "triumphal march" of progress—all of them realistically painted and accurately detailed—which the contemporary middle-class viewer would be able to recognize and identify with, and from which he or she could derive inspiration and reaffirmation. For example, the paintings depicting Greek and Shakespearean drama would exemplify the proud roots of Austria's current theater.

The subjects of the eleven works executed by Klimt ranged from ancient Egypt and classical Greece to the Italian Renaissance. With his figures in frontal poses and his gold-decorated backgrounds, these paintings anticipate the later work that made him famous.

During these years of hard work and ambition, Klimt also had his first portfolio of drawings published. These painted sketches, including *Fable* (1883) and *Idyll* (1884), alluded to the decorative allegories that would also make him famous—works that would juxtapose naturalism and decorative patterns and create their own social commentaries.

THE AUDIENCE AT THE OLD BURGTHEATER

Klimt was already getting a solid reputation among the privileged class. In 1888, he completed the painting that would ensure his place among the entire populace of Vienna.

The painting was *The Audience at the Old Burgtheater*, a commission Klimt received from the Vienna City Council. Its members wanted the old theater portrayed for posterity before it was destroyed to herald in the new Ringstrasse Burgtheater. Its last performance was held in 1888—the same year the new Burgtheater, with the Company of Artists' new decorations, was completed.

Klimt did more than merely paint a view of the inside of the old theater. Using the stage as his "eye," he painted its audience. Here, settling into their seats after intermission, excited and anticipatory, are the upper middle-class citizens of Vienna depicted with photographic realism. It is as though Klimt is saying that the central point of theater is not what's happening on the stage, but what's going on among the tiers of seats. With this naturalistic, carefully delineated painting, Klimt is asserting that this scene is true historical drama in the making—with the upper middle-class audience in the leading role. He implies that this new upper middle-class is far more important than the fictional drama being represented on stage—and, equally important, that they know it. The painting caused a sensation among the Viennese citizens. In 1890 Klimt became the first recipient of the new Imperial Award from the Hapsburg Emperor. He also, most likely, received a number of requests for copies of the painting from those illustrious citizens who were depicted.

Klimt's fame was spreading. He became a member of the esteemed Co-Operative Society of Austrian Artists. Along with his brother, Ernst, and Franz Matsch, he received "the highest possible recognition" for the decorations the Company of Artists did for the Court Museum. And Klimt's name even came up for a professorship at his alma mater, the Academy of Applied Arts. Unfortunately, it was voted down—as it would be three more times during his long career.

But, despite the academics' hesitancy about Klimt's imaginative, slightly unorthodox style, the formidable upper middle-class continued to embrace him. Indeed, his identification with them led to a number of lucrative commissions, including *Portrait of a Lady* and *Portrait of Sonja Knips*—both of which show a combination of almost photographic realism with decorative motifs.

A HIATUS

In the midst of his increasing acclaim, Klimt suffered two great losses. In 1892, his father died of a stroke and, a few months later, his brother Ernst died.

In his grief, Klimt stopped painting for a short time. In 1893 he traveled to Hungary where Prince Esterhazy commissioned him to paint the *Interior of the Theater of the Castle of Esterhazy of Totis*. The prince wanted the painting done in the same style as the *Auditorium of the Old Burgtheater*, with its audience, rather than the stage, the focal point. The castle-theater painting was such a success that it, too, won awards for its artist. In 1893, Klimt was awarded a silver State Medal.

Once again, with this recent recognition of his talent, Klimt's name was proposed as the new professor of historical painting at the Fine Arts Academy of Vienna. And once again, the position was offered to someone else—in this case, the painter Kasimir Pochawalski.

But there was little time to ruminate on the politics of academia. Klimt was soon hard at work on a second portfolio, which was be published in 1895. In this edition of color plates, Klimt included the allegorical studies, *Sculpture*, *Tragedy*, and *Love*.

Love was one of the first paintings where Klimt used his technique of shadowy background figures. Unbeknownst to the realistically drawn embracing couple in the foreground, the shadows hold faces of evil, of old age, of death, even the transient faces of youth. They transport the unknowing couple into the silent conspiracy of life and its sometimes painful path.

But there was more in store for Klimt than published works of allegorical art. In 1894, Klimt, along with his fellow painter Franz Matsch, was commissioned by the Ministry of Education to paint what would turn out to be the infamous Faculty Paintings for the ceiling of the newly constructed Ringstrasse Vienna University auditorium.

THE FACULTY PAINTINGS

The Minister of Culture and Education had high aspirations for the Faculty Paintings. He envisioned the important academic faculties grandly portrayed in allegorical form. The ceiling paintings were to evoke "The Victory of Light Over Darkness," a hymn to rationality, science, and progress.

Klimt presented three preliminary sketches to the Ministry: *Philosophy*, *Medicine*, and *Jurisprudence*. (Franz Matsch did the painting for Theology and a central panel depicting the general theme, *The Victory of Light Over Darkness*.)

All three of Klimt's sketches were very badly received—which was hardly surprising. Klimt had refused to merely celebrate the triumph of reason. Instead, he sketched a dark, romantic world where humanity blindly stumbles through life, a puppet in the control of an impetuous, sometimes dark, force of nature.

Philosophy depicts the mute, impenetrable face of the distant heavens, a backdrop to an endless column of crying humanity, where shadowy bodies swirl in the painterly mist, strong and shriveled, young and old. Although it was not well-received in Vienna, in 1900 the unfinished *Philosophy* won a Gold Medal at the Paris World Exhibition.

When the painting *Medicine* was presented to the University administration in 1901, it was even more vehemently rejected. Here, Hygeia, the Greek goddess of health, is a mysterious enigma—and not the rational, solid figure representing triumph over death. As she stands, arms outstretched and clothed in brilliant decoration, behind her parades a column of women in various stages of life—pregnancy, old age, childhood, and death—intermingled with figures of men, their faces in shadow.

As with the female figures Klimt painted in all three works, Hygeia is the embodiment of woman, elusive and powerful—in opposition to the turn-of-the-century female ideal as someone weak, irrational, and unconcerned with higher education.

This view of the importance of women is given an even more dramatic significance in *Jurisprudence*, also completed in 1907. Here, the accused—frail, naked, and old—is the only man in the composition. He is surrounded by six women, personifying such high ideals as Truth, Justice, and the Law. The women are encased in fluid shapes; they are both a part of the accused and beyond him. Klimt reflects the psychological controversies awash in Vienna at this time, a man threatened by female instincts, a world where public ethics becomes personal pathos.

18

There would eventually be so much ill feeling between Klimt and the university administration that he would buy back the drafts of his paintings in 1905. But, before that date, he continued to work on his compositions for the Faculty Paintings.

ARTISTIC WAVES IN THE NEW MIDDLE CLASS

In fin-de-siècle Vienna, the new middle class was frustrated. The Hapsburgs still retained autonomous power; politics played out between the aristocracy and the socialist and labor parties representing reform and the lower classes. The middle class, with its industry and manufacturing concerns, could not get an effective voice in the Viennese government, which continued to be oriented toward agriculture.

Instead of government, they found their voice in education, culture, and art. They wanted to divorce themselves from traditional forms of art, from the romantic-neoclassical movement and the realistic depiction of historical events.

By the 1890s, Impressionism had become almost staid, an acceptable, even conservative art form in European art circles. Post-Impressionism—freed from the restraints of Impressionism's spontaneity, its emphasis on nature, its imperative to paint what is seen—began to flourish, especially in North European countries, where it was called Expressionism. Vincent van Gogh's angry landscapes, Edvard Munch's profound depictions of human despair, James Ensor's swirling brushstrokes that illuminated the macabre, Henri de Toulouse-Lautrec's emphasis on the seamier side of life— these were personal visions of a world gone mad. The new Expressionists were concerned with emotion, the depiction of angst and confusion, mood and sensation, which they created by using thrusts of bold, discordant color, swirling lines and jutting forms, and abstract perspectives and surreal, symbolic backdrops.

Art Nouveau, which had its roots in Western Europe, in the sensuous, fluid lines, symbolic themes, and exotic, dreamlike work of Aubrey Beardsley, Louis Tiffany, and Rene Lalique, was a more comprehensive approach to art and culture than

Expressionism. It was represented in architecture, furniture, and room decoration, as well as in paintings.

Klimt embraced both Expressionism and Art Nouveau, or the Jugendstil, as it was called in Vienna. In fact, Klimt's name became almost synonymous with the Jugendstil. It was a perfect beginning for new artistic thought, the perfect place for a young, discordant, and frustrated Viennese culture to break away from tradition and begin anew.

The breakaway point was called the Secession—and Klimt became its most forceful spokesman.

THE VIENNA SECESSION

The year 1897 was a frustrating one for Klimt and other artists of the Jugendstil. More and more, their philosophies and styles were at opposite poles with the more traditional artisans of the city. Worse, the Co-Operative Society of Austrian Artists, the organization they had joined in the hopes of finding more artistic freedom, was becoming increasingly conservative and also emphasized the commercial aspects of the applied arts, rather than the artistic, creative element.

Finally, in May 1897, Klimt and a group of forty other artists broke away from the Co-Operative Society and formed their own union: the Vienna Secession. Klimt, the Secession's new president, wrote: "As the governing body must be aware, a group of artists has been trying for years to bring their views on art to bear within the Co-Operative Society. These ideas have culminated in the realization that the artistic scene in Vienna must be brought more vigorously into line with the progressive development of art abroad, that exhibitions must have a noncommercial, purely artistic basis, that this must give rise in wide circles of society to a purified, modern view of art, and finally that official circles must be encouraged to cultivate art to a much greater extent."

The Secession was born. Almost immediately, plans began for a Secession Building to be designed by architect Joseph Maria Olbrich. It was to be a magnificent structure, complete with the

20

The Beethoven Frieze
(detail)

unique feature of adaptable walls that could be moved about to better display a particular exhibition. Above its massive main entrance would be inscribed the words: "To Every Age Its Art, to Art Its Freedom."

The Secession Building was opened in 1898, but, unfortunately, not in time for the Secession's first exhibition—which took place in May and June of that year at the Viennese Horticultural Association Hall. On display were 154 works of art by artists from throughout Europe, including Alphonse Mucha and Auguste Rodin.

Klimt designed the poster for the first exhibition. Graphically depicting "Theseus Slaying the Minotaur," the poster was initially banned by the authorities. After all, it held a powerful message: Theseus, symbolizing the Secession which, in its most daring avant-garde act, slayed its "father"—the traditional culture and values of Viennese society.

But, despite its avant-garde, rebellious nature, the Secession received official approval. The Emperor Franz Joseph actually visited the exhibition and thus gave the Secession immediate credibility.

Further promoting their cause was the Secessionists' magazine. In 1898, the group published its first issue of *Ver Sacrum*, named after an ancient Roman initiation rite for young men, which proclaimed to society at large that romantic notions from the Middle Ages and the Renaissance on would be discounted—and that new, pure artistic ventures would be explored.

But 1898 would prove to offer more than artistic freedom for Klimt. He became an international artist, with membership in the London Society of Painters, Sculptors, and Engravers and in the Munich Secession. And in that year he also made his debut as a landscape artist.

KLIMT'S LANDSCAPES

Klimt's landscapes seem to go on past the picture frame; they never depict human figures or interaction; they are static and yet,

22

at the same time, swollen with anticipation. Although fifty-four paintings out of Klimt's total output of 230 are landscapes, they are not as well-known as they should be.

Klimt painted landscapes during his summer holidays, in the Austrian countryside at Weissenbach and Kammer on Lake Atter, where he was free from the critics and their disapproval. There he could paint a part of his private, inner world that had no political overtones—and could not be attacked on ideological or stylistic grounds.

Although Klimt's first four landscapes—*Orchard, Farmhouse with Climbing Roses, Orchard in the Evening,* and *After the Rain*—are all oddly shaped, the remainder are all painted in a square format. They suggest extreme tranquility, but never lackluster boredom. Indeed, life flows from the geometric perfection of the square format; it streams from the treetops, disguises itself in the reflective surfaces of the water.

In *Fir Woods I* and *Fir Woods II,* the trees escape the viewer's limited field of vision, soaring out of the reach of the picture frame. Others, such as *Roses Among the Trees* and *Farm Garden with Sunflowers,* suggest the decorative patterns of Klimt's other works; they are expressive in their loose brushstrokes, contrasting colors, and ambiguous images; they are almost abstract.

While Klimt continued to work on his Faculty Paintings, escaping from his concentration with summer landscapes, his fame continued to grow—due in no small part to Emilie Flöge, the woman closest to his heart.

PORTRAITS OF EMILIE AND OTHERS

Klimt once said, "I'm sure I'm not particularly interesting as a person." As he had never painted any self-portraits—and as he had kept a quiet, private life—he must have believed this to be so.

But women adored him—and he adored women. He was intrigued by them and, unlike many men of his time, he was not afraid of their power. Indeed, as his Faculty Paintings show, he celebrated it. He found women exhilarating and mysterious and many of his drawings were erotic.

Emilie Flöge was one of the women attracted to Klimt—and she remained with him throughout his life. In 1891, Klimt's brother had married Helene Flöge. Although their marriage did not last, they had stayed together long enough for Klimt to meet Helene's sister, Emilie who owned a fashion boutique with Helene. She knew many influential people and, through her friendships, she helped Klimt get important and lucrative commissions.

Klimt received one of his first and most important private commissions in 1899 from the industrialist Nikolaus Dumba, who wanted Klimt to paint the decorations for the music room in his elegant Vienna. In fin-de-siècle society, the rooms in one's home were places where wealthy residents could retreat, to develop their inner lives. Paintings, decorations, even the clothing a homeowner wore, were all in harmony, all consistent with a general theme.

To that end, in the paneling above the doorways Klimt did two paintings that involved music. *Schubert at the Piano* shows Klimt's abandonment of rigid academic painting. Although it is traditional in its depiction of a historical event, it is far from realistic. The figures are dressed in contemporary clothes. The glowing candlelight reflected in the mirror gives the painting an impressionistic feel of light and space.

Music II, its companion painting, has a completely different style. It is an allegory, filled with symbols and patterns. An ancient sphinx, a Grecian mask, and a woman's face are realistically portrayed in the foreground, but the background consists of a highly decorative pattern very characteristic of Klimt's work.

Between 1898 and 1899, Klimt also painted several important canvases in which he explored the sensuality of women over and above the historical event portrayed. His *Pallas Athena* represents primordial myth and ancient eroticism; in the hand of the gold-armored Pallas is a small standing red-haired nude, her arms outstretched. In the allegorical painting *Nude Veritas*, a red-haired nude stares out at the viewer; she holds a mirror reflecting "truth"; she seems to be trying to say something. There are almost carefree decorative patterns behind her and an inscription above her head reads, "Pleasing Many Is a Bad Thing."

In *Water Nymphs*, also painted in 1899, the women's faces are the only realistic references on the canvas. They seem all-knowing as well as trapped within their fluid, decorative forms. The dark background, the serpentlike shapes, and the flashes of white, suggest the depths of the ocean as well as the mysterious power of feminine eroticism. In light of Freud and his psychological theories, the painting seems to acknowledge the emerging importance and awareness of the unconscious realms of the mind.

By 1901, Klimt was coming into his own. His style was becoming immediately recognizable, with its eroticism expressed in very tightly confined and refined decorative compositions. *Judith I*, for example, shows the Jewish heroine as a seductive siren. Judith saved her people from the Assyrians by killing their general, Holofernes, and cutting off his head. The severed head is barely seen in the right-hand corner of the painting. The rest of the canvas is a rhythmic pattern of luminous goldwork surrounding the realistically drawn Judith—who is sensual, proud, and even innocent all at the same time.

Klimt's *Portrait of Emilie Flöge* shows his emerging decorative style, with its fluid patterns and ambiguous backgrounds, combined with a realistic portraiture that is startling in its emotive expression.

But one of Klimt's most monumental works was yet to come.

THE SECESSION'S BEETHOVEN EXHIBITION

In spring 1902, the Secession held its fourteenth exhibition—which would ultimately mark the high point of the group's success. A staggering 5,800 visitors admired the works of twenty-one artists, all of which were conceptually and spatially organized around a central theme: Beethoven, the artist who was adored unconditionally in the nineteenth century.

The Secession Building, with its moveable walls, was the perfect place to exhibit the artists' work, keeping all unified within the central theme of Beethoven, but highlighting each one as a self-contained piece of art.

Organized by Jugendstil architect Josef Hoffman, the exhibit's main focus was a sculpture of Beethoven by Max Klinger. In order to see the statue and the two flanking frescoes—*Daybreak* by Adolf Bohm and *Nightfall* by Alfred Roller—viewers first had to go through the room where Klimt's *Beethoven Frieze* was shown.

Constructed with poor-quality materials like plaster on trellis-work, the *Beethoven Frieze* was originally supposed to be dismantled at the end of the exhibition. But, ironically, it has outlived many of the other works shown at Secession exhibitions. The Austrian government bought the frieze and, in 1986, after a long, delicate, and costly restoration, returned it to the Secession Building and placed it in a specially built replica of the room it first occupied in 1902.

The *Beethoven Frieze* is an unusual work of art. It not only contains mirror fragments, buttons, and even costume jewelry, but its allegorical message, its composition and form, is shrouded with mystery. The monumental work was inspired by the final chorus of Beethoven's Ninth Symphony, the "Ode to Joy." According to the exhibition's catalogue, the entire frieze depicts allegories of cravings and desires, of swirling, suspended hostilities ready to spring on an individual whose strength and ability to endure pain and suffering make him a hero. The images of woman have varied shapes. She is seen as a witch, a mermaid, a fairy-tale animal, as well as an upper middle-class matron. Men are formed by these women; man's ego and salvation comes from his embrace of both feminine and male ideals. Ultimately, the frieze shows art as humanity's salvation.

The catalogue takes the viewer through the entire monumental work, explaining that the subject of the frieze is the redemption of weak-willed humanity through art and love. The first portion of the frieze, facing the entrance wall, represents the human longing for happiness.

The narrow central frieze continues the theme as it portrays the hostile forces that are responsible for mankind's sorrows, powers that can only be resisted and subdued through art. Depicted is Typhoeus, the mythological giant, and his three Gorgon daughters, who represent disease, madness, death, nagging grief, and other evils. Above them, mankind's aspirations soar and glisten beyond their reach.

The final portion of the frieze portrays the transforming power of art, which "leads us into the kingdom of the ideal, where alone we can find pure joy, pure happiness, pure love." A female figure is shown embracing the hero, her body almost entirely obscured by his. Their faces are hidden as they merge into a total loss of personal identity, and they find redemption in their unified love.

RISING STAR

The *Beethoven Frieze* brought Klimt such fame that in 1903, the eighteenth Secession exhibition was entirely dedicated to his work. He showed thirty drawings and forty-eight paintings, including *Jurisprudence*, one of his infamous Faculty Paintings.

Klimt's art was becoming more and more distinctive. He had honed his decorative, Byzantine-mosaiclike patterns to a masterful art form, combining gold and brilliant color, tendrils of fluid forms, carefully designed repetition, and realistically composed portraiture to create great works of art—allegories that are always symbolic and ambiguous.

Hope I of 1903 is an example of Klimt's definitive style. The painting shows a naked woman in an advanced stage of pregnancy; she is in profile, her arms folded across her stomach. Her long red hair and the fixed, almost shameless expression in her eyes make the painting erotic. She seems unaware of the skull and the three sinister-looking women in the background.

With its portrayal of a pregnant woman who seems naive of life's vicissitudes, *Hope I* was considered so unorthodox that it was not exhibited for a full year after completion. The Secession members were afraid of kindling the same kind of controversy Klimt faced with his Faculty Paintings. Even

Klimt's often used red-haired model, Herma, hesitated before agreeing to sit for the painting.

Hope II, painted four years later, was the complete antithesis of *Hope I*. As erotic as the pregnant woman was in the first painting, here she is totally lacking in sexuality. She is partly clothed; she does not meet the viewer's gaze. Indeed, her entire stance is one of resignation, a foreshadowing, perhaps, of the Great War that was soon to come.

A NEEDED BOOST

By 1904, the Secession was in trouble. The group itself was dividing along two lines, between those, like Klimt, who believed in the importance of the applied arts and called themselves Stylists, and the Realists, who felt they wanted more artistic expression. They were losing favor—and interest—among the public.

First the Secession magazine *Ver Sacrum* ceased publication. Then the Austrian government withdrew its unconditional support. Finally, the Ministry of Education rejected the Secession's request to participate in the 1904 St. Louis World Fair.

The final blow came when the Klimt Group was renounced for putting commercialism above art—the same reason the Secession first split from the Co-Operative Society years before. The commercialism claim was not unfounded. One of the lucrative projects that Klimt participated in was the Viennese Workshop, co-founded by architect Josef Hoffman. The workshop united several artistic disciplines, including gold-, silver-, and metalwork, bookbinding, and cabinet-making, under one roof. The Workshop was highly successful—and commercial. It later became the impetus behind Viennese modernism, an artistic, spiritual, and philosophical movement exemplified by the combination of function and art, science and artistic expression, in one.

Another commission further antagonized the noncommercial Realists camp: the *Stoclet Frieze,* begun in 1907. Thanks to industrialist Adolphe Stoclet, the Secession artists were about to have their dream of a visionary, global work of art—without economic restraints or critical interference—come true. Stoclet's Palace in Brussels needed to be decorated and the Austrian group was asked to submit their ideas. Architect Josef Hoffman designed Stoclet's new home; Klimt was asked to create the mosaics for the enormous dining room walls.

The *Stoclet Frieze* was not completely finished until 1911. Made of costly materials, including gold, brass, ceramics, and semiprecious stones on marble panels, it is a modern masterpiece. The mosaic itself, with its Byzantine influence, consists of fourteen panels, divided into two parts: *The Wait* and *Fulfillment*. Unlike the *Beethoven Frieze*, the design elements of *Stoclet* take precedence over any message. It is the sumptuous material, the elaborate lines, and the abstract images that create their own message: that of luxuriant ornamentation.

The *Stoclet Frieze* could never be accepted by the noncommercial Realists in the Secession. Armed with their successful Vienna Workshop, Klimt's Stylists group decided to resign. In their subsequent letter of resignation, they wrote: "Artists . . . should endeavor to extend their influence to more and more areas of modern life. Indeed, they are obliged to make use of any opportunity which offers itself in order to promote the life of art in the broadest possible sense."

This new artists' association, informally called the Klimt Group, had their first exhibition in 1908. It was the first time the public saw what would become Klimt's most famous work of art.

THE KISS

The Kiss, widely reproduced even today, is considered the most popular painting in Klimt's Gold Period (so named because of his extensive use of gold paint and gold-leaf ornamentation). In *The Kiss*, a man and a woman on their knees embrace while completely encased in a radiant golden mist. Their bodies are only distinguishable by the decorative patterns on their robes; one merges with the other. The man's gown is decorated with rectangles; the woman's with circles within circles.

The Kiss captures the embodiment of union; it portrays a total fusion between man and woman, pure, delightful, and erotic. *The Kiss* was sold almost immediately for an impressive twenty thousand florins.

The second Klimt Group exhibition took place in the summer of 1909. Here, the two emerging Expressionist painters Egon Schiele and Oskar Kokoschka also showed their work. They were very much influenced by Klimt, by the way he captured sensuality and expressed it within strict confines.

Klimt was making way for other artists. By 1917, he had become a mentor not only for Schiele and Kokoschka but for other new artists. He had been made an honorary member of the Academy of Fine Arts in Vienna. He had also become a renowned international figure, exhibiting in Rome, Dresden, Venice, Munich, and Budapest.

On January 11, 1918, Klimt suffered a stroke in his Vienna apartment and died. On his deathbed, he supposedly said, "I want Emilie to come." He was fifty-six years old.

Unfortunately, many of Klimt's great works, including his Faculty Paintings, were destroyed by fire in 1945. But his legacy lives on through his unique vision and comprehensive approach to art. His paintings are both mysterious and accessible, full of beautiful images, appealing decoration, and allegorical meaning; and his leadership of important early twentieth-century art organizations helped to make art a part of life for a wide public. Klimt's popularity, in his own time and in ours, is an indication of the success of his vision of timeless beauty and meaningful art.

HIS WORKS

Love

Love (detail)

Love (detail)

Fable

Fable (detail)

Fable (detail)

·IDYLLE·

Idyll

Idyll (detail)

Idyll (detail)

The Auditorium of the Old Castle Theater

The Auditorium of the Old Castle Theater (detail)

The Auditorium of the Old Castle Theater (detail)

Portrait of a Young Woman (detail)

Portrait of a Young Woman

Sonia Knips

Sonia Knips (detail)

Pallas Athena

Pallas Athena (detail)

Water Nymphs (detail)

Water Nymphs

Franz Schubert at the Piano (detail)

Franz Schubert at the Piano

Judith I

Judith I (detail)

Judith I (detail)

Beech Wood I

Emilie Flöge

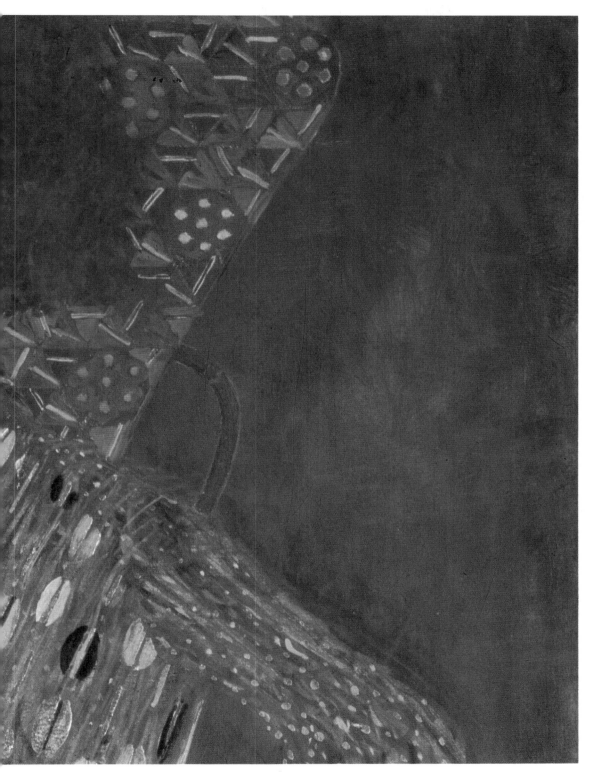

Emilie Flöge (detail)

Emilie Flöge (detail)

Water Snakes I (Friends)

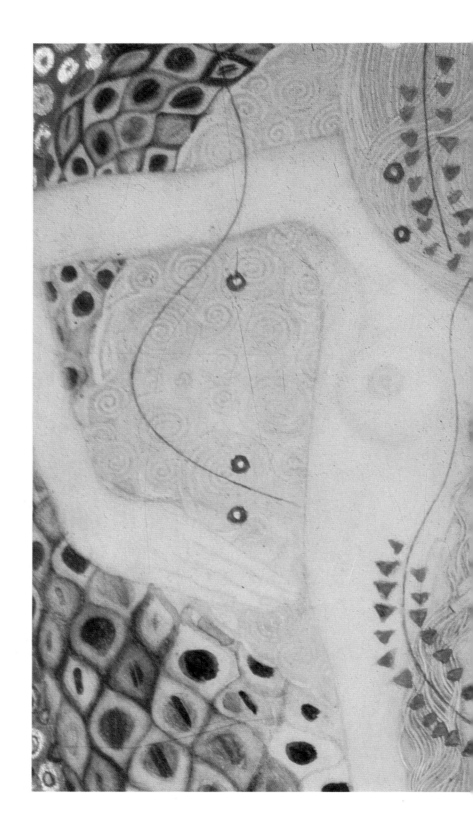

Water Snakes I (Friends) (detail)

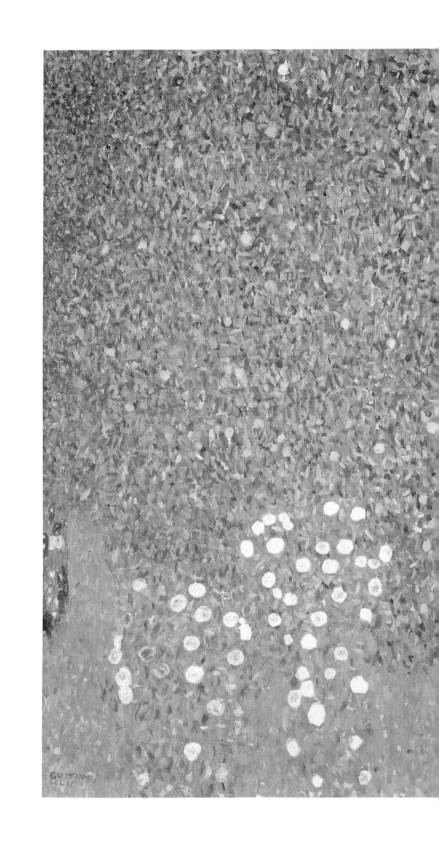

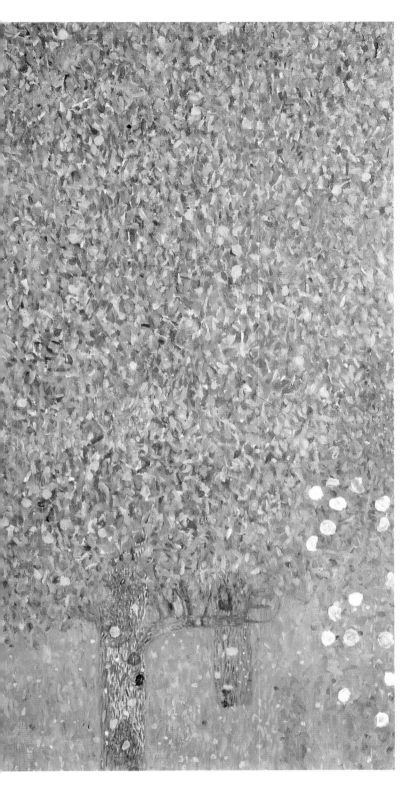

Roses Among the Trees

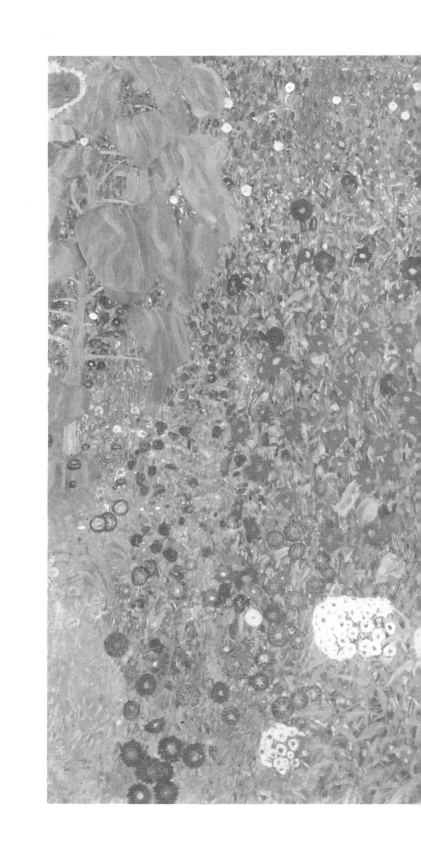

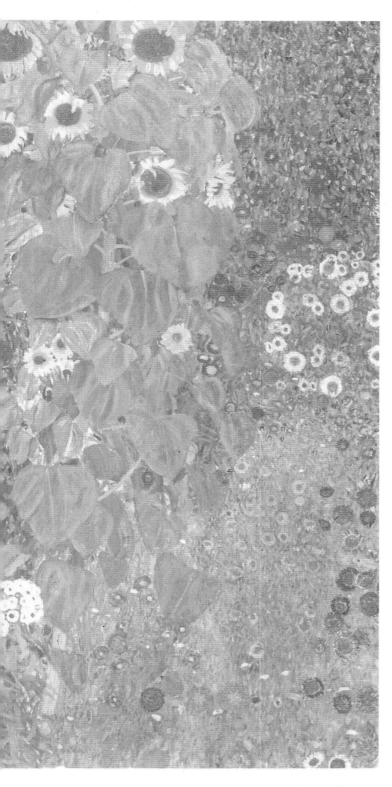

Country Garden with Sunflowers

Fritza Riedler

Fritza Riedler (detail).

Fritza Riedler (detail)

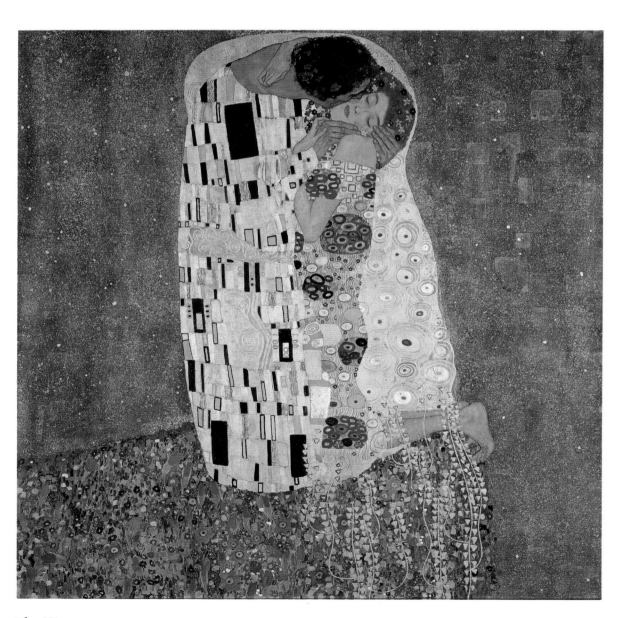

The Kiss

The Kiss (detail)

Judith II

Judith II (detail)

Judith II (detail)

Full-Face Portrait of a Lady

Full-Face Portrait of a Lady (detail)

Portrait of a Young Woman

Portrait of a Lady

Portrait of a Lady (detail)

Stampa Grafiche Editoriali Padane Cremona